A VISIT TO MONT SAINT-MICHEL

When you finally reach this mythical monument whose silhouette has been visible for miles, it is easy to imagine how impatient pilgrims must have felt back in the days when a long and difficult journey across these dangerous strands finally brought them to the foot of Mont Saint-Michel to earn their paradise, after facing all the perils of the road.

Today, the dyke makes it a lot easier to get to but it has also caused the area around the Mount to silt up. So advocates of heritage conservation have obtained permission from the authorities to demolish it and convert it into a footbridge allowing the incoming tide to restore the Mount's island nature. Legend has it that the sea submerged the forest of Scissy (an idea disputed today), leaving three rocks, Mont Tombe, Tombelaine and Mont Dol, sticking out.

Today, you enter "this fortress of faith" through the outer gate made in a barbican of the rampart after the bastion of the Tour du Roi. This wall around the Mount was built up progressively as artillery developed, indeed we should not forget that until the early 16th century, only cannonballs were fired, not explosive shells. This outer gate takes you into the

main street of Mont Saint-Michel. In military architecture, as we know, the gate is seen as a point of weakness in the bastion, so Mont Saint-Michel is guarded by a succession of three gates, the outer gate, the boulevard gate, and the third one, the Porte du Roy with its drawbridge.

The outer section today contains the tourist information office where visitors can find out everything they want to know about the Mount, not least of which a copy of the indispensable "tide tables", to avoid getting into difficulties in the bay and car parks. The cannons standing in this courtyard are English mortars from the Hundred Years War, called Michelettes.

From this courtyard and going into the Grand'rue, I discover the lower village of the Mount! For this holy place is in fact made up of two villages one above the other, the first one, the "town of Mont Saint-Michel" with its parish church, its shops and cemetery, and its town hall, is completely independent from the

second, more spiritual and even monastic one, which also has its church, the abbey church, and its cemetery, for the monks… To go from one village to the other or even to explore the first village, there are several possible routes, each of which is very different in character.

The first one is suitable for the energetic or those in a hurry and who do not have a heart condition. It completely ignores the main street and the museums, which, between you and me is a bit of a shame, as each of these are interesting aspects of the Mount.

To take this route, just after the post office, before the house called "La Confiance", on the left you go up a steep set of steps straight to the gardens, the only place on the Mount where you can have a comfortable shaded or even romantic picnic. Then, passing in front of the history museum, you take the steps on the left to get onto the Grand Degré (big flight of steps in Old French) from where you can reach the 'pit' leading to the abbey.

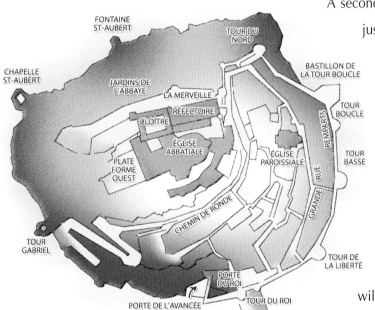

A second route goes up the steps to the right, just after the Porte du Roy, from where you can go up onto the rampart and the Tour du Roy which has a magnificent 180° view from Grouin du Sud to Brittany. This view gives you a sense of the dangers of the access routes, at the mercy of quicksands and the sea. The secrets of these routes are known only to the guides who will also tell you about the flora and fauna of this remarkable place.

The third route is for those of an inquisitive turn of mind or for the pilgrim who, before gaining his paradise through this pilgrimage, would give in to the final worldly temptations in the village, eating and feasting before making his confession and accomplishing all the rites of faith in the abbey. Today, the visitor with plenty of time on his hands and wishing to make the most of his visit can go into the 4 museums and explore the shops and restaurants on his way up to the abbey. A range of catering is on offer between the "Mère Poulard" (the first restaurant you come to) and the "terrasses Poulard" at the end of the street. There is something for everyone to choose according to their tastes and budget.

The expanse of the bay, an immense open space, calls to mind a desert, and as in a desert, the calm is only apparent and often unsuspected dangers threaten the unwary walker. Guides are on hand to help you, and their knowledge makes their informative, protective and sometimes life-saving presence essential. Indeed, this bay, beneath its natural beauty, conceals a great many dangers, the least obvious of which is probably the thunderstorm, which you might think more of a problem up in the mountains, but on an apparently flat stretch of land the slightest elevation attracts lightning and this is the main reason why the guides keep a close eye on the weather forecasts.

The tide flows in and out of the bay twice a day which causes shifts as far as the riverbeds, creating pockets of water or quicksands. These sands are areas close to the bank where sea-sand mixes with the water; under foot, the soil reacts like a carpet laid on jelly, into which you sink more or less quickly depending on the thickness of the upper layer which forms a kind of crust.

These quicksands disappear and reform as a result of the intermingling of the sediments with the tides and the rain. Only people used to these salt flats are able to recognise the affected areas. Finally, what with storms and tides, the occasional fog doesn't help matters either. So, you should never venture out into the bay without a compass and without having checked the tide tables and the weather forecast, the best thing is to use a guide who knows the routes of the bay.

You should realise that to get to the Mount, you have to cross at least two rivers, the Sée and the Sélune. During your excursion in the bay, guides will tell you about its very rich wildlife. The bay is a conservation area in which 150 to 200 species live or gather, including the Shelduck, a large black and white duck. You can tell the male by the bump on its red beak and the brown-yellow band on its breast. In winter you can watch Brent Geese which nest in Siberia or Greenland, and many waders such as the Eurasian curlew. The Genêts cockle, flatfish, sole and plaice are to be found in the sand. The guides will be delighted to tell you all about these as well as about the geological formation of the bay.

The maritime museum on the Mount is also an excellent source of information on the marine life of the area.

Nowadays, guides also lead pilgrimages on foot across the salt flats to the Mount from Genêts and Saint Léonard, from Courtil and Beauvoir, as in days gone by.

Guides can also take you from the Mount to Tombelaine. At the start of certain walks in the bay, you cross the salt meadows now reserved for sheep, whose meat is highly prized because of this type of grazing. You will still sometimes see horses and cows in the wettest places. This was once the domain of geese raised for their down. A return trip takes 4 hours 30 minutes without commentary and 5 hours 30 minutes with, both trips of course including a stop at the Mount.

The bay is silting up and a major project is under way to restore the insular character of the Mount. The reason the bay has silted up is because the sea takes five to six hours to rise and approximately an hour longer to go down, which leaves a sedimentary deposit exacerbated by the presence of the dyke-causeway. This will be replaced by a bridge, the car parks will be moved from the foot of the Mount to Beauvoir, and mechanical flushing systems will be introduced. With this set of measures, careful studies have shown that the Mount could once more be surrounded by water at high tide. Whether this is achieved remains of course to be seen when the work is finished.

A guided tour of the area around the Mount is the best way to understand the way construction progressed alongside the development of military techniques, especially artillery. Turning your back on the sea and raising your eyes to Saint Michael all shining with gold, you can see the triple architectural symbolism, on three levels. These three levels correspond to the three strata of medieval society:

- At the bottom, those who toil.
- In the middle, those who govern, reign, fight, kings and knights.
- At the top, those who pray, here, the monks.

In the beginning, the Mount was occupied by canons, who were secular priests (not in an enclosed order). They were driven out in the 10th century because of "misconduct", and substituted by monks of the Order of St Benedict who came from the abbey of Saint-Wandrille (near Rouen).

The Maritime Museum: This first museum is entirely devoted to the sea and its environment, in the bay in which the Mount is the gem. Here you can see boats, from the drakkar to the clipper and other steamships. You learn about how the tides work and the role of the rivers, and the enormous mass of water involved: over a million m3! You learn about the salt meadows known as "herbus", their flora and the wildlife of the bay, the polders useful to man at the expense of the insularity of the Mount, and the project to return it to its natural state.

Archéoscope: This is a very well-documented show with impressive light and sound effects, designed to reflect the faith and the essential magic that prevailed during the construction of the Mount. It shows the history of this citadel to God, never captured, the stages of its construction, the logical order of things, the great events of history, the spiritual perspectives for each person to interpret in their own way.

After this museum, if you want:

- to go onto the ramparts, go through the shop called "La fée des grèves" on the right.
- to go to the abbey, take the cemetery steps on the left, which will take you to the gardens and then the abbey.

VISITE HISTORIQUE

95 — MONT SAINT-MICHEL. L'Entrée du Mont à Marée haute. ND Phot.

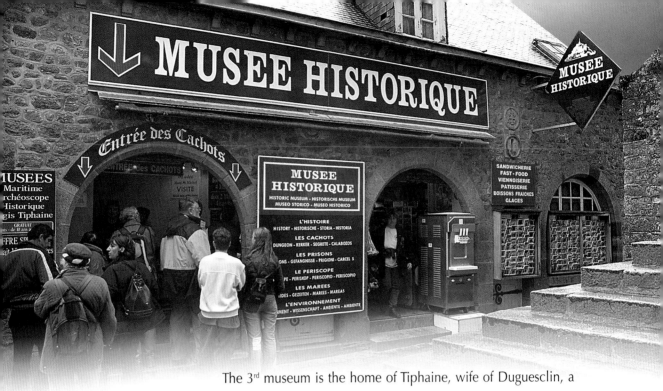

The 3rd museum is the home of Tiphaine, wife of Duguesclin, a woman ahead of her time. Leaving to serve the Dauphin, the future Charles V, Bertrand Duguesclin, Captain of Pontorson and the Mount, left his wife Tiphaine, who was keen on astrology, at home. In a carefully created setting, you are taken back to this period with its overtones of rigidity but also with its special aura of chivalry, and its environment. All the furnishings and décor are interesting. Here you

discover a very different Tiphaine from the woman you might imagine all too often trapped, at that time, by certainties and prohibitions…

The 4th museum: the history museum, in the tradition of Mont Saint-Michel waxworks museums, tells the heroic deeds, adventures and life of the men who made the Mount.

A commentary recorded by Philippe Noiret, a highly talented actor, relates the stories of Mont Saint-Michel great and small, in a highly detailed scene inhabited by waxwork figures. Here you will also learn that the Mount, turned into a prison, housed Raspail and Blanqui before the latter was elevated to the Senate. In a different vein, you learn about the rule of St. Benedict: Ora et labora (pray and toil!) and all it implied…

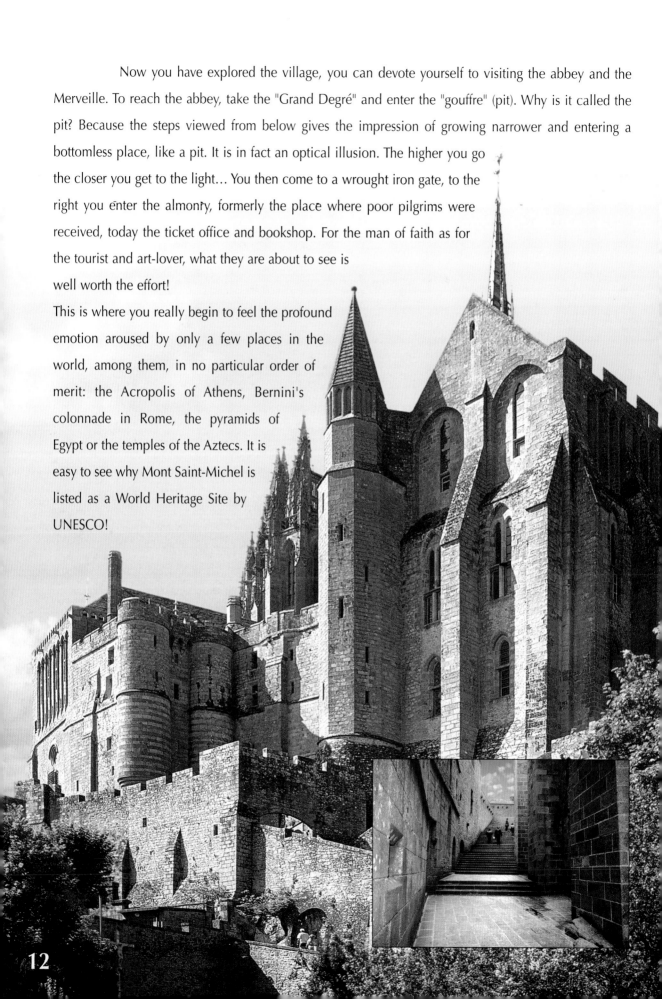

Now you have explored the village, you can devote yourself to visiting the abbey and the Merveille. To reach the abbey, take the "Grand Degré" and enter the "gouffre" (pit). Why is it called the pit? Because the steps viewed from below gives the impression of growing narrower and entering a bottomless place, like a pit. It is in fact an optical illusion. The higher you go the closer you get to the light… You then come to a wrought iron gate, to the right you enter the almonry, formerly the place where poor pilgrims were received, today the ticket office and bookshop. For the man of faith as for the tourist and art-lover, what they are about to see is well worth the effort!

This is where you really begin to feel the profound emotion aroused by only a few places in the world, among them, in no particular order of merit: the Acropolis of Athens, Bernini's colonnade in Rome, the pyramids of Egypt or the temples of the Aztecs. It is easy to see why Mont Saint-Michel is listed as a World Heritage Site by UNESCO!

Above the flight of steps, after the entrance gate, which leads you to the level of the abbey, two footbridges overlook you one after the other. The first, an open one, gives access, from the abbey building on the left as you go up, to the room known as "Belle Chaise", the courtroom where the abbey, which also had jurisdiction over some of the surrounding areas, dispensed justice.

The second one, roofed and enclosed, formerly gave access to the south transept of the abbey church, but is today used for the Mount's administrative offices.

When you reach the top of the steps, you can see the water tank on the right and, on the left, the entrance to the administrative offices and you come to a small square known as Saut-Gaultier (Gaultier Leap), named after a lovelorn prisoner who leapt to his death.

Once across the Saut-Gaultier, you come to the abbey parvis or west terrace. What a view! We are at a height of around 80 metres. From there, you can get a sense of the original size of the abbey…

Let us begin our tour with a bit of history…

14

In 966, Richard I, grandfather of William the Conqueror, drove out the canons and replaced them with Benedictine monks from Saint-Wandrille. These, in the great purpose of constructing a building that might respond to the influx of pilgrims, wanted a construction worthy of the glory that must be rendered to God. Sadly, the rock did not provide a sufficient base! So they decided to build out towards each of the four points of the compass buildings in the form of chapels, which would form the platform on which the future building would stand. In the majority of Christian churches, the main entrance is to the west, facing the setting sun, the chancel is situated in the east, towards the rising sun, representing Christ, the sun of the world. Thus we have, beneath the chancel in the east, the great pillared crypt, in the south, the Saint-Martin crypt, in the north, the crypt of Notre-Dame des trente cierges and in the west Notre-Dame-sous-terre (Notre-Dame-sous-terre and Notre-Dame des trente cierges can only be visited on guided tours).

In the oldest crypt (Notre-Dame-sous-terre), the remains of a pre-Romanesque church have been found, perhaps the first shrine built on the Mount?

Before going in, to the left of the abbey, on the parvis, the library occupies the former monks' dormitory. The dormitory was next to the church in order to meet the requirements of the rule of St. Benedict, which obliged the monks to get up during the night for matins and primes. The monastic day was punctuated by prayers, periods of meditation and contemplation, leaving room for some work and the meals taken together in the refectory, twice a day.

On this square, if you look closely at the stones on which you are treading, you can see marks made by the stone-cutters (piece-rate workers); these were used to measure their work so that their payslips could be drawn up. They also made it possible to establish, if any problem arose, who had done what. Finally, for each stone-cutter, this mark was proof of his work.

You then enter the nave which is worth a few explanations. Indeed, it was shortened in the 18th century, after a fire destroyed the first three bays. The ruins were taken down and the new façade built at this level, which is the reason for certain differences in level of the terrace. A fine example of the Romanesque-Norman style with its semicircular arches, the building consists of three floors, which is unusual for the early 11th century, and gives the whole a rare harmony, as at Jumièges, Saint-Ouen in Rouen (Seine-Maritime), and Lessay in La Manche. But the vault had to be made lighter and so it was built out of wood instead of stone to enable it to be supported by the side walls in spite of its height.

Continuing the tour of the abbey church, after the transept, whose right arm houses the organ, you find seven radiating chapels. In the chancel you can see a hole in the paving that communicates with the great pillared crypt.

The Romanesque chancel collapsed in 1421… This was during the Hundred Years War which meant that the construction of the new chancel was not begun until the early 16th century, in the Gothic style of the period.

Above the transept crossing is the lantern tower, whose neo-Romanesque base represents celestial Jerusalem, open to all sides. On its spire, which is neo-Gothic, stands the Archangel Michael. The present statue, the work of Parisian sculptor Frémiet, a bronze lightning conductor 2.70 metres high, can be dismantled and is gilded in fine gold. Its installation by helicopter, following restoration, was broadcast worldwide.

Beneath this spire, at the transept crossing, you will see a wooden statue of the Archangel Michael striking down the dragon.

Leaving the transept, you go out of the abbey church on the right-hand side and enter a courtyard, enclosed on the left by the monks' dormitory, and then into the cloister "a true Marvel". This part of the building is indeed known as the "Merveille" or marvel. The quincuncial arrangement of the colonnades is of a rare beauty and extreme delicacy, the wooden structure, the work of marine carpenters, is elegant and refined. The chimney flues you can see come from the lower floor, from the scriptorium.

When the king of France conquered Normandy, sowing ruin and desolation, he gave a lot of money to the monks to redeem himself! So in the early 13th century, in just 17 years, the monks built the Merveille: cloister and colonnade in a succession of tripods, archways made from limestone from Caen decorated with friezes of flowers, columns in lumachel from England (Salisbury, Canterbury), which have now been restored after erosion by weather, with pudding stone from La Lucerne. This cloister symbolises the level of meditation, food for the soul.

246 — Abbaye du MONT SAINT-MICHEL. La Merveille (XIVᵉ s.). Tympan du Cloître.   ND. Phot.

From this marvellous cloister, you enter the monks' refectory, a place for fraternal feasts, during which, in his throne on the right, the designated monk would read the bible, the rule of St. Benedict or holy books to his brothers.

The Merveille was the project of the monks at the time the funds were received: "We are going to represent the three levels of medieval society in three adjacent buildings, each building will have three storeys, and each storey will include a large room with symbolic and social significance, the figure three representing the Holy Trinity and the three social levels of the Middle Ages".

But the funding was not enough to cover the whole project and only two sections were successfully completed, the west Merveille: - cloister (food for the soul), scriptorium (food for the spirit), cellar (food for the body) - and the east Merveille: - refectory, guests' hall, almonry.
The third Merveille, never built, was to comprise, from top to bottom, the chapter house, library and stables.

In their community, the Benedictine monks lived according to the rule established at the monastery of Monte Cassino by their founder St. Benedict (Ora et labora), 8 hours of prayer, 8 hours of intellectual work and 8 hours of manual labour. What room did that leave for sleeping and eating? The sixty monks (the maximum number for Mont Saint-Michel) met together twice a day for their meal of bread, vegetables and wine (the latter had two functions, to nourish and to warm). The rule even stipulated the quantities of wine and whether it was to be drunk neat or watered down. The meal also sometimes included fish, as Mont Saint-Michel was an island. Meat was restricted to bipeds (poultry), otherwise fish and meat were reserved for festivals or for the sick.

As you go through this refectory, you have the strange impression of seeing the windows opening before you and closing behind you; in addition to this optical effect, designed by the 13th century architect, a symbolic meaning and excellent acoustics were created.

From the refectory, you go down to the guests' hall, which was where royalty was received. In the passage, half-way down on the right, you will see a depiction of the appearance of the archangel to St. Aubert, the bishop of Avranches.

As soon as you enter this hall, you sense a much less austere atmosphere; three fireplaces, two for the kitchen and one at the side, no longer there, for heating. A dumb-waiter enabled dishes to be sent between the guests' hall and the monks' refectory.

In this dining room, equipped with latrines, feasts were held and notably meats were eaten that were roasted in the two immense hearths, easily big enough to cook an ox, and which were separated from the dining room by a hanging or tapestry suspended from a beam resting on two corbels facing one another, which you can see between the two doors. The very slender perspectives draw the eye upwards towards the heavens.

The room is composed of two bays supported on polygonal based pillars (Norman style), the capitals are decorated with acanthus leaf carvings. If you close your eyes, you can imagine this hall paved and decorated! All this has now gone … On the right, looking towards the end of the room, is an oratory, the St. Madeleine chapel.

Those received in this hall were members of the "family" of the Mount, in other words the donors. To save their sinning souls, they gave generously to the monks, providing them with significant resources to maintain and embellish the Mount. "This family" was understood in the widest possible sense as these guests would invite their friends and relations.

On the Mount, levels are rarely constant, and we should never forget that we are on a rock whose original shape has in most cases been followed, so you have to go up in order to go down, next, to the scriptorium

This scriptorium, or writing room, was the cultural centre in which scribes, but above all copyists and draughtsmen, illuminated manuscripts, some of which can still be seen at the town hall in Avranches, twenty kilometres from the Mount. This room was erroneously referred to for a time as the knights' hall.

The scriptorium was not enclosed, and therefore open to certain lay people and heated by two fireplaces between which a gallery circulates in the wall. This gallery contains period latrines! In the middle of the room, a trapdoor gives access to the storage cellar. Here, we return to monastic austerity, with massive columns on polygonal bases. Note the protruding astragal (a narrow moulding at the base of the capital), and the acanthus leaf sculptures which are very deep. The overall design is conducive to contemplation and a strong reflection of the monastic conception of architecture which was intended to contribute to guiding one's thoughts.

Pilgrims were not admitted into this room. The hall, light today, did not look like this originally. The large window at the end of the room corresponds to the passageway to a room of the third structure, the library, which was never built. From the scriptorium, you can either go back to the almonry and the exit or visit the foundations of the platform, the four Romanesque crypts, although only the Saint-Martin crypt in the south, and the great pillared crypt in the east, can be visited without a guide.

To get to the crypts and for the reasons already explained, you have to go up in order to go down, which is one of the phenomena that make the Mount puzzling to the visitor.

1925 MONT-St-MICHEL
Le Promenoir, xii° siècle, ou ancien Cloitre
construit sous les ordres de Roger II

Cliché A. V.   Collection L. G. B., Saint-Pierre-Église

Leaving the scriptorium, you can go straight up and return to the level of the abbey church and the cloister.

On the right, you come to a vaulted room, the covered walk, which is pure Romanesque, but with a vault with early Gothic elements (heavy pillars but vault in pointed arches to take the strain off the walls). This part does pose some difficulty to archeologists who, generally, set the beginnings of Gothic art in 1144, with the chancel of the Saint-Denis basilica near Paris. But this would make Mont Saint-Michel the forerunner! What, perhaps, gives credence to this view is the unorthodox support of the vaults, suggestive of an early architectural experiment. Another interesting feature is the solid columns.

We are now on the north-south stairway (beneath the west terrace with the entrance to the abbey church). Down a short flight of stairs, we find on our right a first access door to the apartments of Robert de Torigny, famous Abbot of Mont Saint-Michel in the 12th century. The main entrance is down a further flight of stairs.

Going down these stairs, on the left, we come to the entrance door to Notre-Dame-sous-terre, one of the chapels serving as a base for the abbey church. This is not open to visitors today, except on guided tours.

Further on, you come to the Saint-Etienne chapel after passing in front of the apartments of Robert de Torigny.

This was the monks' funerary chapel, where the last tributes were paid to their bodies. It followed the infirmary and preceded the cemetery-ossuary. However, monks prepared for the final end did not fear being taken into the infirmary for there you ate better, and it was warm. There they were bled to take away the humours in order to purify the soul and the body.

In this funerary chapel, on the base of the altar, you will see alpha and omega, the evangelical symbols of the beginning and the end. To the right of the altar, a niche in the wall held the oils with which to anoint the dying; to the left, looking towards the altar, a pietà: the Virgin contemplating the body of her crucified son, resting on her knees.

To the left of the altar, the south entrance door of Notre-Dame-sous-terre. Going out of the chapel, you come to one of those wheels that was used to carry heavy loads up to the upper floors. This one dates from the period when the Mount was a prison. It was used to bring up provisions and equipment for the work of the prisoners. Wheels, no doubt similar to this one, were used to hoist the granite stones from the îles Chausey during the construction of the Mount, but they were moved, like scaffolding, as the work progressed and especially when there were changes of level.

At the end of this area, there was originally no wall, but a space where the bodies of deceased monks were buried. Their bones were then recovered and placed in an ossuary in order to make room for the next to die.

Leaving this room and going past the tank (which you could see as you climbed up to the abbey), you reach the Saint-Martin crypt. This southern crypt supports the south arm of the transept of the abbey. Here you can see double transverse rib arches, so-called because they double the vault. Next you come to the great pillared crypt to the east, which supports the chancel of the abbey church; originally Romanesque, it collapsed in 1421, destroying the vault of the crypt as it fell.

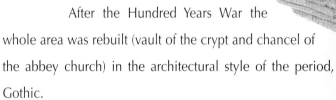

After the Hundred Years War the whole area was rebuilt (vault of the crypt and chancel of the abbey church) in the architectural style of the period, Gothic.

The crypt's enormous pillars support the chancel which is 28 m high. In the vault of the crypt you can see the trapdoor into the chancel for raising the bells, at least so it is thought. On the floor of this crypt, you will see fragments of mosaics which have been interpreted in various ways… Finally, if you are wondering about the reason for the central pillars, they are designed to support the heavy weight of the chancel.

From this crypt, you go down to the almonry, where in former times, pilgrims would eat… the leftovers from the monks' meals!

Immediately adjacent, the cellar that was once used to store wine and drinks is now the exhibition hall, where you can see the plaster model for the statue by Frémiet of the Archangel Michael that dominates the Mount, entirely gilded with fine gold.

As you go out of the cellar, you come into the gardens which were the site for the third building, never constructed. From these gardens there is a very fine view over the bay and Tombelaine.

Going along the outside walls of the Merveille and looking upwards, you can clearly see the three levels: the windows with single openings are those of the almonry; the double windows correspond to the guests' hall; the triple windows to the refectory. This route takes you back to the Grand Degré from where you can either go down via the ramparts from the north tower, or via the main street where you can shop, have a drink or a meal.

Like all abbeys, the abbey of Mont Saint-Michel grew rich and extended its power thanks to donations from the Duke of Normandy and other lords anxious to save their souls burdened with heavy sins from a life of debauchery and war; thanks also to donations from pilgrims who made the Mount, already 1000 years ago, the 4th most important place of pilgrimage in the west, after Jerusalem, Rome and Santiago de Compostela.

Like all abbeys, the Mount was able to weave a quite remarkable web of relationships and professional contacts. In the heart of this bay with its abundant fish, sole and flatfish, salmon on their way back up the Sée and Sélune rivers, shellfish and crustaceans, the marine world contains plenty of treasures today harnessed by shellfish breeding, especially on the Breton side. The land is not to be outdone, with butter, eggs, cream, pigs, poultry, sheep and salt-meadow lambs all produced in the region.

Every abbey had guest quarters and obtained supplies from its farmers. A flow of trade was thus created between the Mount and its immediate region, both in Normandy and Brittany. Like the abbey, the inns got their supplies from producers at the markets.

196 LE MONT-SAINT-MICHEL. — Mme Poulard,
faisant son omelette. — LL

During the restoration of the Mount, the architect Corroyer, who directed the work, came there with his entire household, as was the practice of the time. Not finding the guest quarters to his liking, he set up his cook, Annette Boutiaut, as an innkeeper at the Mount; she later married a certain Victor Poulard and in 1888 opened an inn known as "La Mère Poulard", which became famous the world over, as it still is today.

The region is rich in produce that Annette Poulard, like her fellow innkeepers, used to prepare tasty recipes. The countryside provides eggs, poultry, veal, beef and lamb from the salt meadows (known as "agneau de pré salé"). The fish-filled bay provides sole, place and shellfish, and salmon is fished in the estuaries.

So, given this abundance and riches, why the omelette?

It was the easiest "impromptu" dish to prepare at a time when pilgrims would arrive without warning across the salt flats. It was eaten either as a starter while the rest of the meal was cooking, or was the dish for the poorest pilgrims, or the dish for everyone during times of fasting and abstinence!

This omelette has caused a lot of ink to flow and its secret is well-kept. There are even gourmets who claim it to be unrivalled.

On the Mount, numerous hotels and restaurants await you along the village street. There is plenty to choose from according to your tastes and your pocket! A place to combine fine eating with a spectacular location.

44

1936 — MONT-St-MICHEL - Côté Sud ou de l'arri

LE MONT-SAINT-MICHEL.
La Grande Rue. — The Street

AU GRAND BAZAR
ENTRÉE LIBRE

-MICHEL.
...oulevard. — ND Phot.

Collection L. G. B., Saint-Pierre-Église

Adresse : HUET, à l'Hermine

Mont-Saint-Michel

45

And so everyone, whether pilgrim, simple visitor or art enthusiast, makes their way back to their daily lives, their head filled with memories and their eyes still wide from taking in this unique splendour. Bon voyage, my friend! You will never forget this rock turned into a marvel and that this gem, by the grace of a river, the Couesnon, is well and truly part of this region of which the humorist Alphonse Allais said "it is fine there several times a day", Normandy.

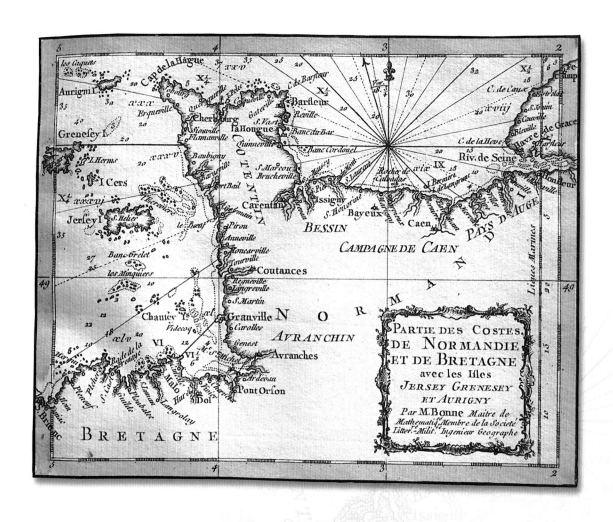

Text: Michel Delauney.
Photos: Éditions Normandes Le Goubey.
Y.R. Caoudal for pages 2 (b) - 5 - 24 and 25 - 42 - 43 and back cover (a)
M. Hasdenteufel for page 20 (a)
With special thanks to the Société MÈRE POULARD; to Mme Nicolle for making available
old postcards from her private collection

ÉDITIONS NORMANDES LE GOUBEY
50 A, Route de Bretagne - B.P. 43
14760 – BRETTEVILLE-SUR-ODON
Tel: 02 31 74 40 40 - Fax: 02 31 73 42 00
Produced by LECONTE

Translation: Gilla Evans for ILS Paris
ISBN: 2-9514995-5-8